Series 117

This is a Ladybird Expert book, one of a series of titles for an adult readership. Written by some of the leading lights and outstanding communicators in their fields and published by one of the most trusted and well-loved names in books, the Ladybird Expert series provides clear, accessible and authoritative introductions, informed by expert opinion, to key subjects drawn from science, history and culture.

The Publisher would like to thank the following for the illustrative references for this book:
Page 5: © Roger Viollet/Getty Images; page 7: © CORBIS/Corbis via Getty Images; page 25: courtesy of Fallschirmjäger via Wikimedia Commons; page 51: © Universal History Archive/Getty Images

Every effort has been made to ensure images are correctly attributed; however, if any omission or error has been made please notify the Publisher for correction in future editions.

MICHAEL JOSEPH

UK | USA | Canada | Ireland | Australia
India | New Zealand | South Africa

Michael Joseph is part of the Penguin Random House group of companies whose addresses can be found at global.penguinrandomhouse.com

Penguin
Random House
UK

First published 2018
001

Text copyright © James Holland, 2018

All images copyright © Ladybird Books Ltd, 2018

The moral right of the author has been asserted

Printed in Italy by L.E.G.O. S.p.A.

A CIP catalogue record for this book is available from the British Library
ISBN: 978-0-718-18630-2

www.greenpenguin.co.uk

Penguin Random House is committed to a sustainable future for our business, our readers and our planet. This book is made from Forest Stewardship Council® certified paper.

Blitzkrieg

James Holland

with illustrations by
Keith Burns

Ladybird Books Ltd, London

On Monday 21 August 1939, Nazi Germany signed a non-aggression pact with the Soviet Union. Politically and ideologically, the two countries were natural enemies, but the USSR was not ready for war, and Adolf Hitler, the German leader, wanted to invade Poland without risk of being attacked from the east in turn. Both countries understood this was a temporary treaty of convenience. It did, however, pave the way for the outbreak of the Second World War.

The following day, Tuesday 22 August, Hitler called together his senior commanders to the Berghof, his house near Berchtesgaden in the Bavarian Alps, and outlined his plans for war against Poland. Since 1919, the enclave of East Prussia, still part of Germany, had been cut off by a narrow strip of land known as the Danzig Corridor. It was time, he told them, to take it back, and to test German military strength. 'We are faced,' he said, with his usual black-and-white world-view, 'with the harsh alternatives of striking or of certain annihilation sooner or later.' The only choice remaining was to crush Poland.

A day later, Hitler announced that the invasion would be launched in a matter of days. Curiously, that evening the Northern Lights were showing over the Alps and a shroud of deep red was cast over the Untersberg. The Führer and his followers were watching from the terrace as the same red light now bathed their faces and hands.

Hitler turned to one of his military adjutants and said, 'Looks like a great deal of blood.'

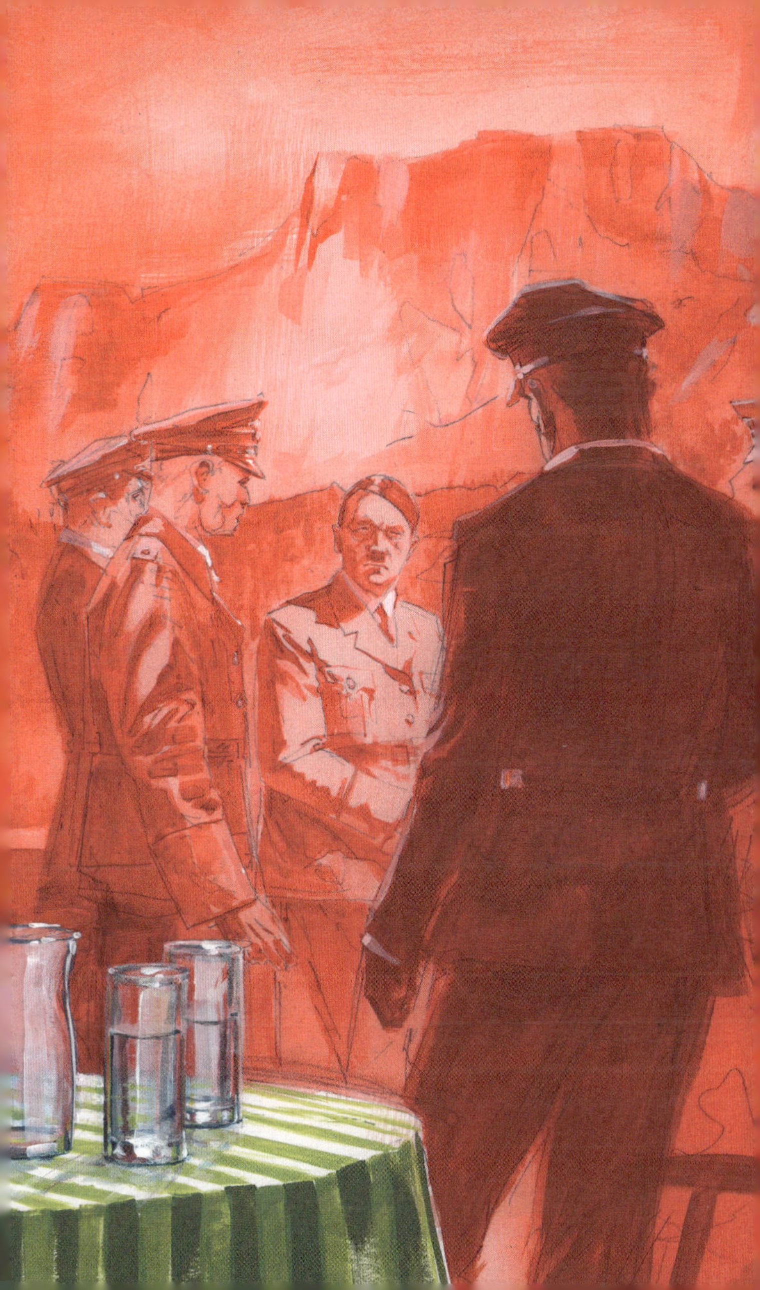

Britain and France, two of the world's most powerful nations, had vowed to defend Poland's sovereignty. This meant that if Germany invaded, then they would both declare war. Many senior commanders in the Wehrmacht, the German armed services, believed this threat, but Hitler thought they were bluffing. After all, in 1936 he had marched back into the Rhineland, ceded from Germany after the end of the First World War, and the French and British had done nothing. Then, in spring 1938, his forces had poured into Austria and brought that country into the Third Reich without a shot being fired; and that autumn, German troops had occupied the Sudetenland of Czechoslovakia, then six months later had taken control of the entire country. Once again, the rest of the world had sat back and watched. Now, in the late summer of 1939, he could not imagine Britain or France risking war over Poland.

In Germany, Hitler's popularity had never been higher. He had created jobs, grown the armed forces, given the German people back their pride, and had taken back all the German-speaking territories, and more besides, without any opposition.

Most Germans also believed that much of Poland was rightfully theirs. Certainly, much of the western part of the country had been within Germany until Poland had been recreated following the end of the First World War. Many there spoke German rather than Polish. Nazi propaganda also told the world that Poles had been carrying out atrocities against Germans.

German troops greeted by enthusiastic crowds during the Anschluss of Austria.

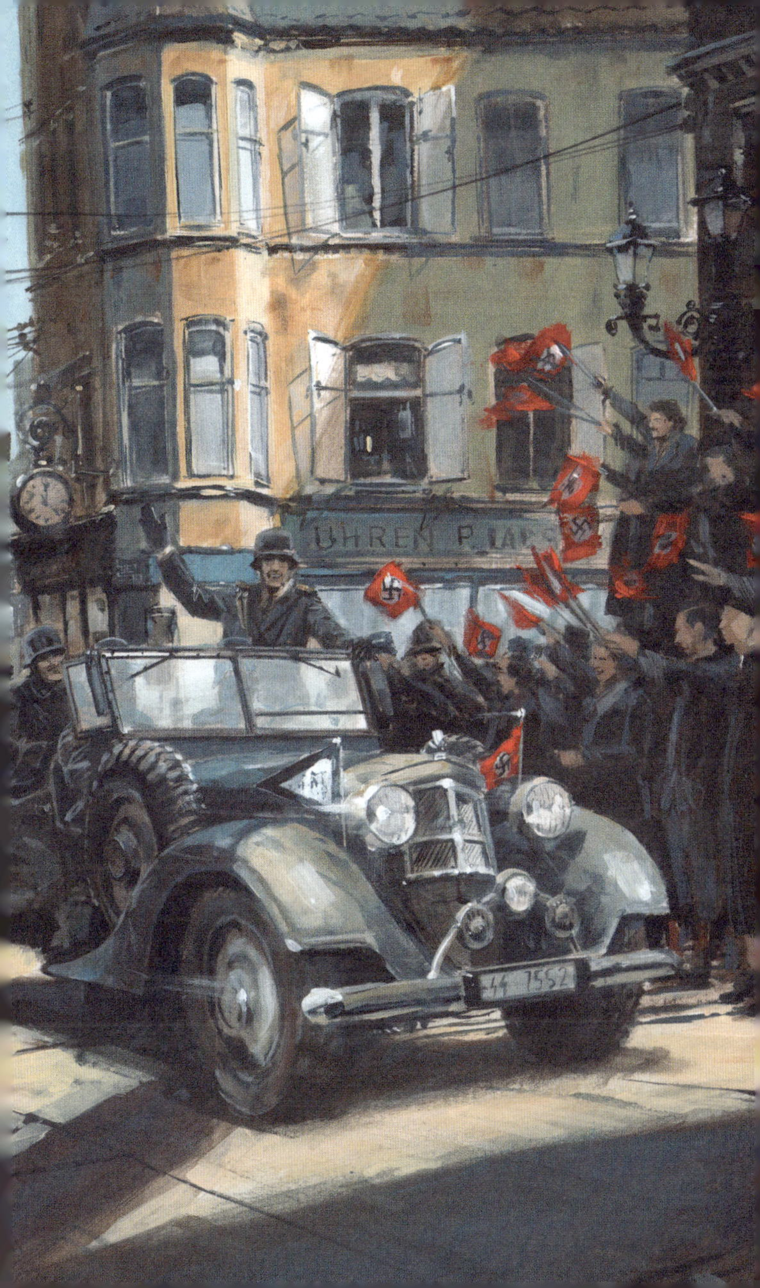
UHREN
7552

Propaganda had been a key component of Nazi strategy from the outset. To a large degree, this was due to Dr Josef Goebbels, the Reich Minister for Popular Enlightenment and Propaganda. It was Goebbels who whipped up hatred of Jews – anti-Semitism – and Communists, as well as convincing the German people of the rightness of Hitler's ambitions. Key to this was repetition and the new media of radio and film.

Goebbels recognized that radios, especially, were an ideal way to get a message across. Germany lagged behind other leading nations in many innovations of the age, but not when it came to radios, which were made in large numbers and cheaply, too. By 1939, almost 70 per cent of the population owned radios, and most were the DKE, or *Deutscher Kleinempfänger*, the 'German Little Radio'. Small and affordable, this ensured there were more people with a radio in Germany than in any other country in the world, including the USA. Public squares, restaurants and bars were also fitted with speakers from which the radio could be heard. 'Repeat, repeat, repeat,' was Goebbels' mantra. Over the airways, on film and in newspapers, the state-controlled media were able to bombard the German people with the same messages: Hitler's genius, the rightness of German territorial ambitions, the growing strength and invincibility of the German armed forces, as well as virulent anti-Semitism and anti-Communism.

And it worked. 'The anger that I felt inside at their unreasonableness,' Lieutenant Hajo Herrmann, a young bomber pilot, said of the Poles, 'matched my sacred conviction: that of German rightness.'

A German family listens to their DKE, the 'German Little Radio'.

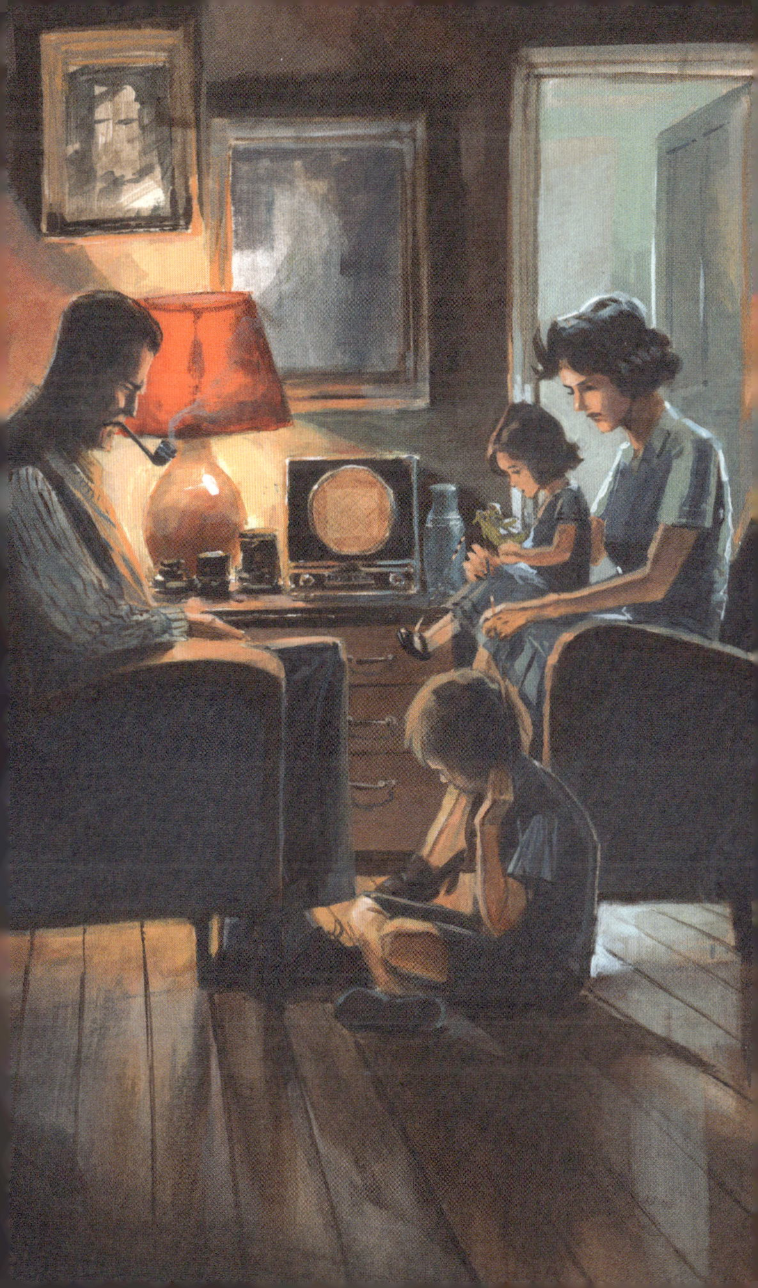

Hajo Herrmann was one of the many bomber pilots in the Luftwaffe – the German Air Force – flying over to attack Polish targets in the early hours of Friday 1 September 1939. On the ground, troops poured over the border. Artillery boomed, panzers – tanks – rumbled forward, while Stuka dive-bombers screamed down, sirens wailing, to drop their bombs. Two days later, on 3 September, Britain and France honoured their pledge to Poland and declared war on Germany.

The German plan was to use the Luftwaffe as aerial artillery, hitting at cities, communications, military targets and also airfields and aircraft on the ground, and so effectively paralyse the Polish defence. The Polish Air Force was much smaller in size and for the most part lacked modern aircraft. Hajo Herrmann and his colleagues were able to destroy much of it in a matter of days.

The German Army attacked in three separate thrusts, all of them driving towards Warsaw, the Polish capital. Despite some stoic Polish defence, the Germans were closing in on the city just eight days after the campaign had begun, with the Poles falling back to the south-east.

On 17 September, Soviet forces invaded from the east, as earlier agreed with Germany, and Poland's fate was sealed. With Warsaw and other towns in ruins, the last resistance capitulated on 28 September. Even so, sweeping aside a militarily weak country like Poland was one thing, but beating two super-powers like Britain and France would be another altogether.

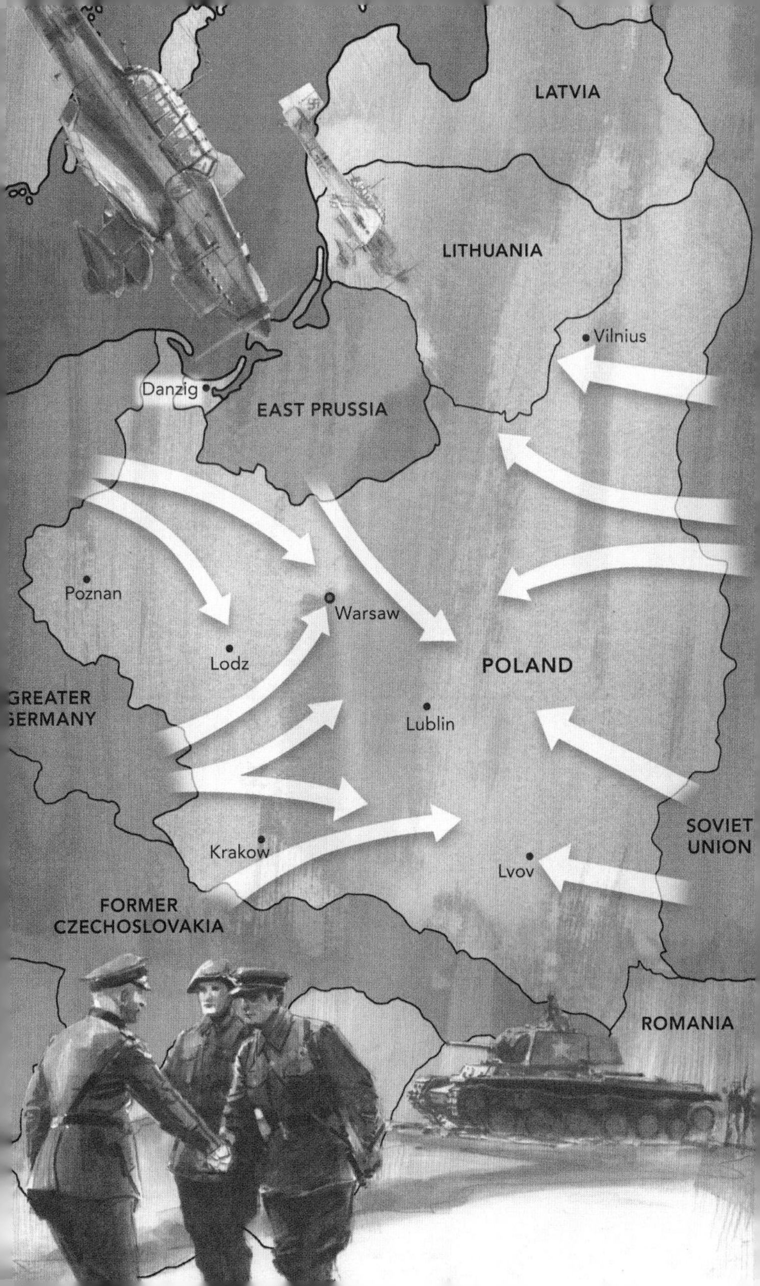
LATVIA
LITHUANIA
Vilnius
Danzig
EAST PRUSSIA
Poznan
Warsaw
Lodz
POLAND
GREATER
GERMANY
Lublin
Krakow
SOVIET
UNION
Lvov
FORMER
CZECHOSLOVAKIA
ROMANIA

On 27 September, with Poland destroyed, Hitler called together all his senior commanders and told them to get ready for an immediate attack in the west against France and the Low Countries. No one said a word in protest, but there were many among them, not least General Franz Halder, the chief of staff of the army, who understood that Germany's armed forces were nothing like as strong as they needed to be to take on Britain and France.

Propaganda had depicted Germany as a giant, modern, mechanized force, better trained and equipped than any other on earth. The reality, however, was rather different. It was true that, in the Luftwaffe, Germany had the largest and best-equipped air force of any country, but France alone had a larger army, with better and greater numbers of tanks, and considerably more artillery. Britain, meanwhile, had the largest navy and merchant shipping fleet, with access to more than 80 per cent of the world's merchant shipping. Its empire was also the biggest that had ever been known. Both Britain and France had ready access to the world's oceans and with it to the kind of resources needed for war.

Germany, on the other hand, lay at the heart of Europe. Her limited access to the world's sea lanes lay in a small strip into the North Sea, now blockaded by the Royal Navy, and ports on the Baltic Sea. It had no direct access to any ocean.

Hitler shocks General Franz Halder by demanding an immediate attack on the West.

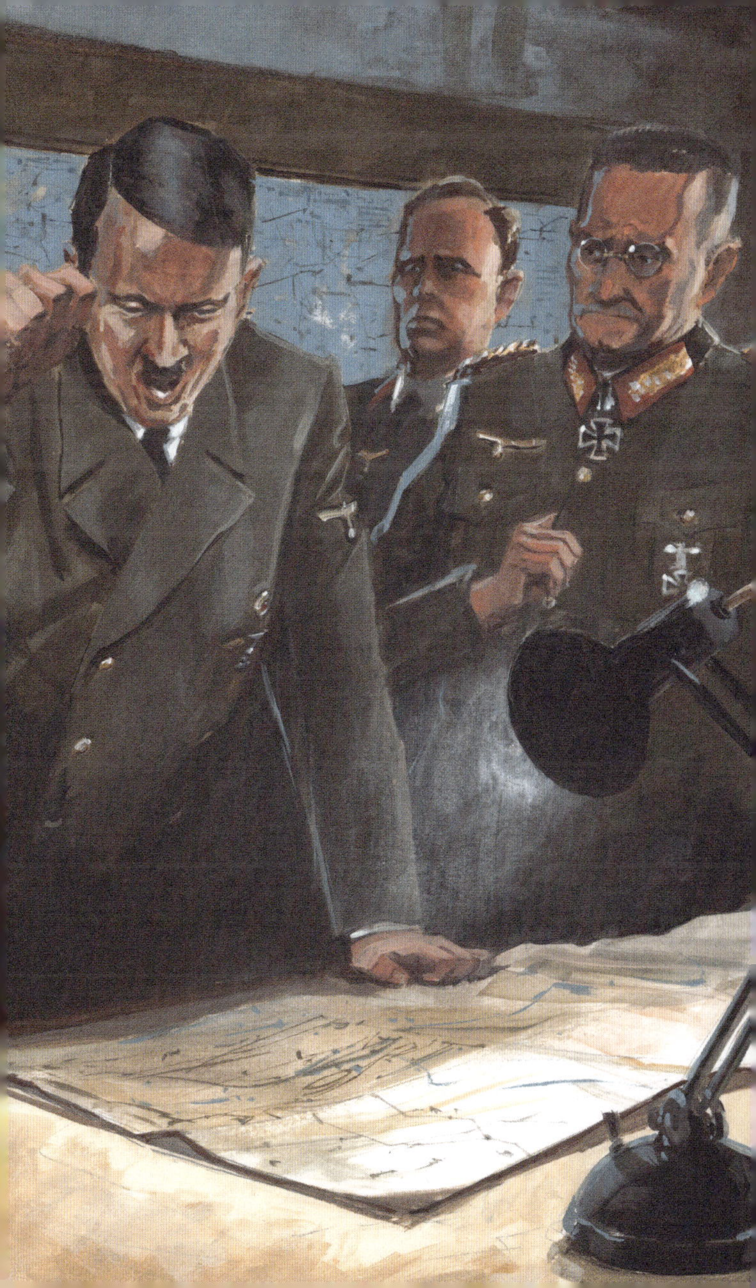

Despite these clear advantages and despite the fact that the vast majority of Germany's military forces had been ploughed into the Polish campaign, neither Britain nor France had ever had much intention of taking the offensive on behalf of the Poles. Britain had a small army, which meant that France would have to take the primary role in any land operation across the border into western Germany. In any case, the British Army was still in Britain when war was declared.

General Maurice Gamelin, the Commander-in-Chief of the French Armed Forces, had, however, promised back in May that French forces would come to Poland's rescue. It was one of the reasons the Poles had earlier resisted any diplomatic solution. Now that war had been declared, Gamelin ordered what he called an 'offensive reconnaissance' into the Saar region of Germany. Nothing happened very quickly, however, and when the French did move, they rumbled just 5 miles across the border, then stopped. By this time, Soviet troops had invaded Poland from the east and the country had been all but destroyed. The French then pulled back behind the Maginot Line, the massive fixed defences that lined the Franco-German border.

A golden opportunity to hit the Germans at their weakest had gone begging. Instead, Britain and France planned to play for time. However, German geographical isolation and economic limitations suggested they would opt for a rapid and decisive attack in the west before too long. The Allied strategy was to withstand this initial attack, continue to build strength, then strike back.

French troops move into the Saar.

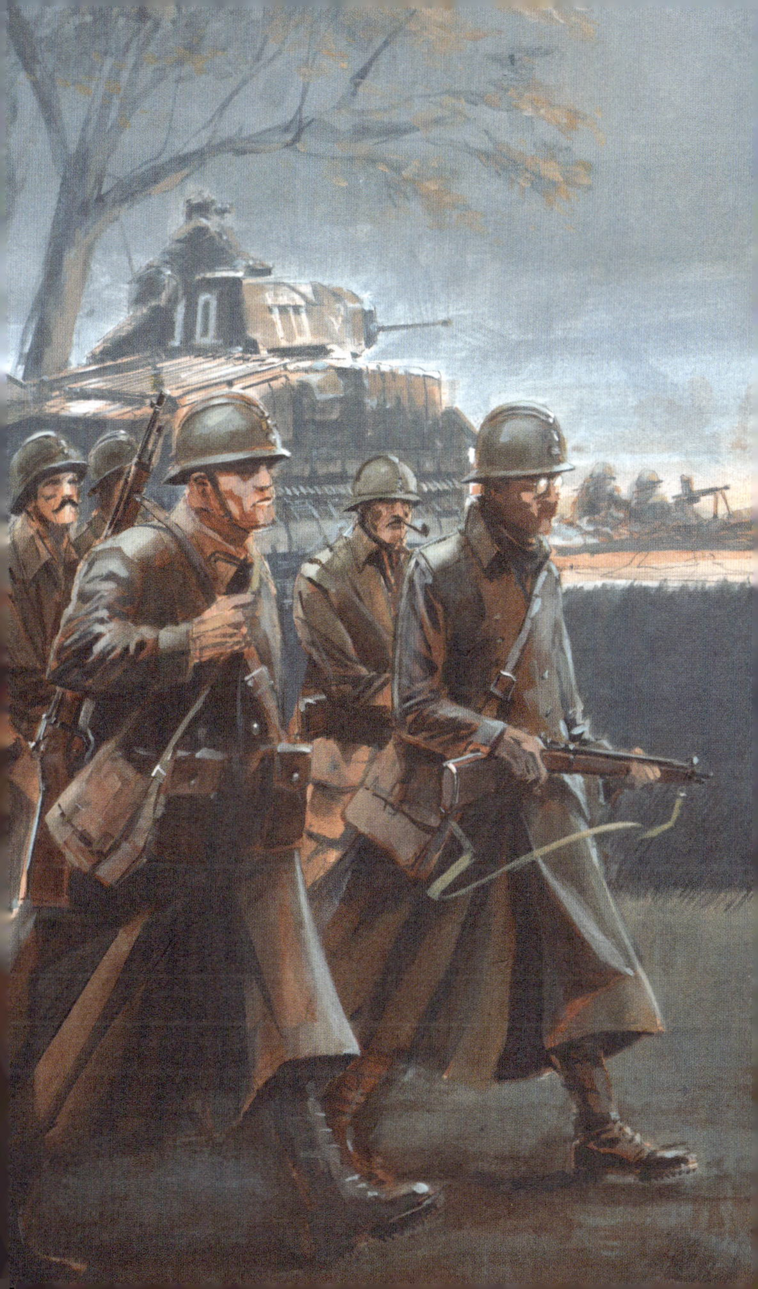

Insecurity lay at the heart of the French military leadership, and they certainly believed Germany to be far stronger than was the reality. In August 1938, for example, General Joseph Vuillemin, the head of the French Air Force, had been invited to Germany to inspect the Luftwaffe. He was shown lines of bombers and fighters and watched them take off and land again, then was driven to another air base, where, unbeknown to him, the same aircraft had arrived just ahead of him. Returning to France, he told the French Prime Minister that, if it came to war, the French Air Force would be annihilated in days. In fact, Britain and France together had more aircraft than the Luftwaffe.

Nor was Germany anything like as mechanized as propaganda suggested. On the eve of war, there was one motorized vehicle for every forty-seven people in Germany, but one for every fourteen in Britain and one for every nine in France. For the invasion of Poland, just fifteen German divisions of the fifty-four used were mechanized. The rest had been dependent on horses, carts and the soldiers' own two feet, which was how German troops had moved for centuries.

Nor was this about to change any time soon, because there were not enough factories, spare parts, mechanics or drivers. Perhaps most importantly, nor was there enough fuel. Germany was, and would remain, extremely short of oil and, without access to the world's oceans, there were limited ways of getting hold of it.

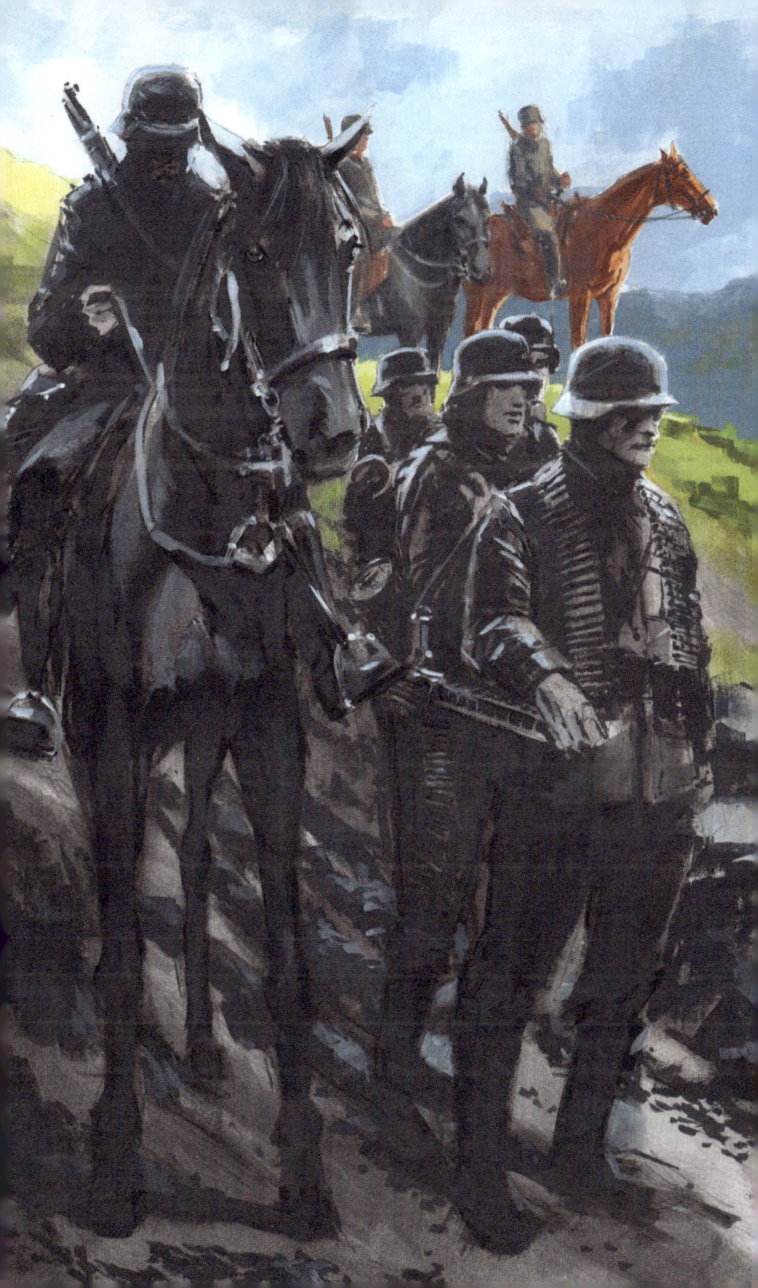

The shortcomings of the German Army were all too apparent to many of its senior commanders, including General Halder, who was now supposed to devise a plan of attack against the West in a matter of weeks. The vehicles they did have had taken a battering on the rough Polish roads, but, even worse, the army had almost entirely run out of ammunition. Furthermore, the fighting in Poland had shown shortcomings in training in many of the German divisions. The division was the military unit by which most armies were judged and tended to contain around 15,000 men, including infantry, artillery and support troops.

By producing a succession of highly unimaginative plans of attack, Halder incurred the wrath of Hitler, but did ensure there could be no immediate assault on the West. It was true that British and French factories would be continuing to produce arms over the winter, but Germany needed to do the same. Only with replenished stocks of ammunition and more trained troops could the Germans have a hope of success.

They also needed a plan of attack that might give them a chance of victory, and Halder knew his current proposal to march into the Low Countries as they had in 1914 was not the answer. Then, in January, two German officers made a forced landing at Mechelen in Belgium and were promptly captured, along with Halder's current plans. This changed everything.

The Messerschmitt 108 carrying Halder's plan crash lands near Mechelen in Belgium.

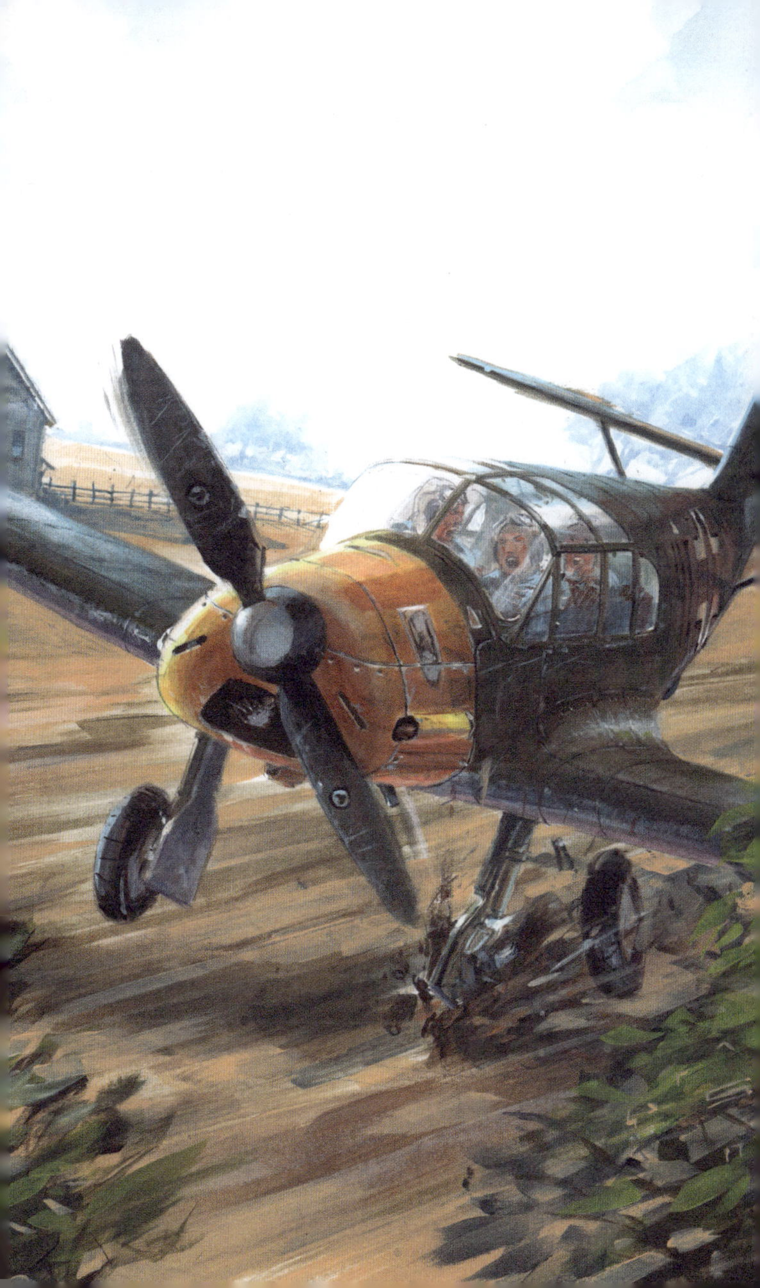

The Allies responded by carrying out extensive troop movements along the Belgian border, all of which were watched by Luftwaffe reconnaissance planes. What at first had seemed an intelligence disaster now looked like giving Germany a glimmer of hope.

Not only did the Allies clearly expect an attack through the Low Countries, but French troop movements had been very slow. This suggested that if German forces could move with greater speed, and in a way the Allies were not expecting, they might be able to catch them by surprise.

Halder now reconsidered a different plan that had been proposed by General Erich von Manstein, but which he had earlier rejected. This was to launch a feint attack into the Low Countries, which would draw the Allies north. Meanwhile, the bulk of the few precious panzer divisions would sweep through the hilly and wooded Ardennes Forest, then drive in behind the advancing Allies in a giant encirclement.

As it happened, von Manstein's plans had also reached Hitler, who had embraced them immediately. Even better, as far as Halder was concerned, the Führer was now talking about attacking Denmark and Norway first. This meant the attack in the west would be launched even later, with better weather and longer days, which would make moving through the Ardennes easier. It was still an enormous gamble, but it was the only plan that Halder could see having even the slightest chance of success. Furthermore, while British and French rearmament had continued, the German Army was now in much better shape, with ammunition stocks replenished and more men properly trained.

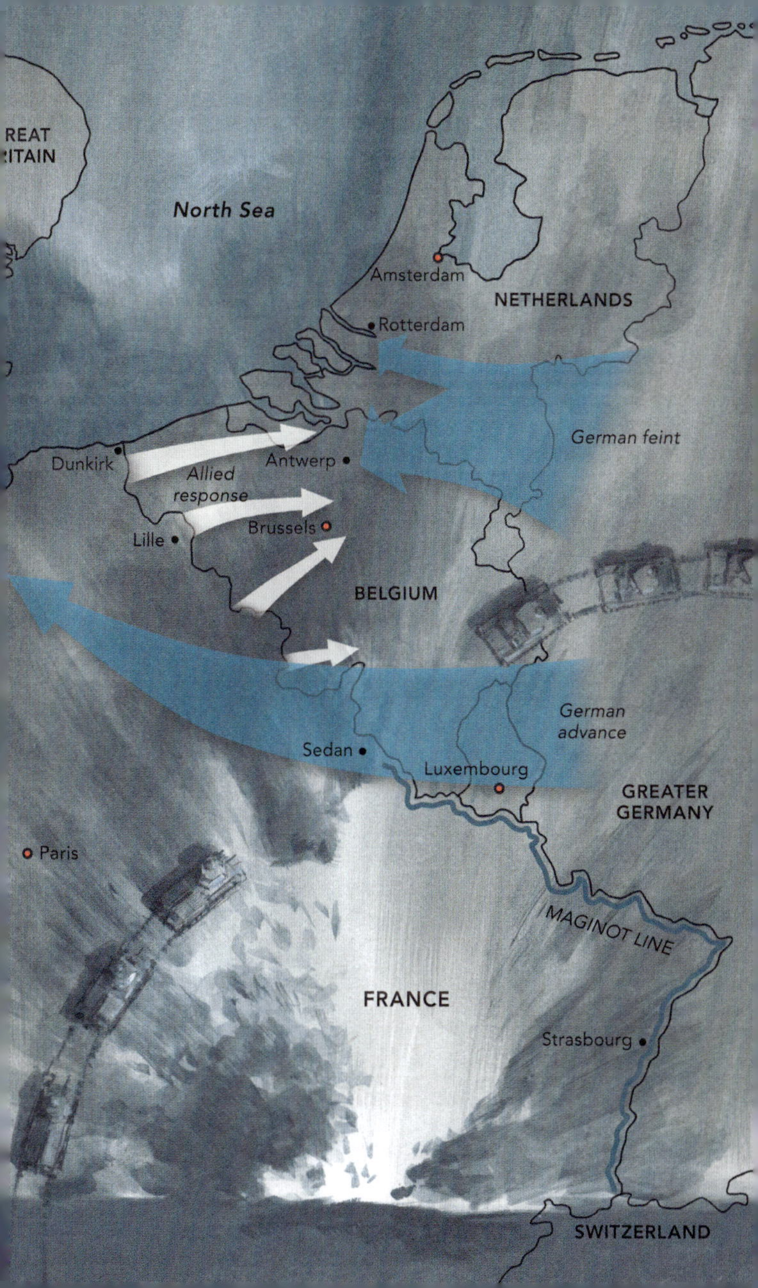
REAT
:ITAIN
North Sea
Amsterdam
NETHERLANDS
Rotterdam
German feint
Dunkirk
Antwerp
Allied
response
Brussels
Lille
BELGIUM
German
advance
Sedan
Luxembourg
GREATER
GERMANY
Paris
MAGINOT LINE
FRANCE
Strasbourg
SWITZERLAND

In actual fact, a drive through the Ardennes was hardly original. The Prussians had passed through the same area in 1870 in the war against France, and again in 1914. Furthermore, the German way of war was always to try to strike hard and fast, knock their enemy off balance and then complete a rapid encirclement before the opposition forces had recovered. This approach went back to the early eighteenth century and was because of the fundamental vulnerability of the country's geographical position in central Europe and because of its shortage of natural resources.

Although the principles of striking hard and fast have come to be termed 'Blitzkrieg' – lightning war – it was not a conscious doctrine for the Germans. Rather, they called it *Bewegungskrieg*: war of rapid manoeuvre.

What was different in 1940 was the machinery and equipment they were using. Germany now had the Luftwaffe to help the spearhead of any attack and provide aerial artillery. They also had tanks. And, perhaps most importantly of all, they had radios: small and easy-to-manufacture radios that could be fitted inside a panzer or even on a motorcycle sidecar.

Despite these advantages, the senior command of the German Army was mostly filled with men who secretly believed Germany had little chance in any battle against the Allies and who had little understanding of how this new technology might be applied. But there were a few exceptions, and one of those was a dynamic panzer general called Heinz Guderian.

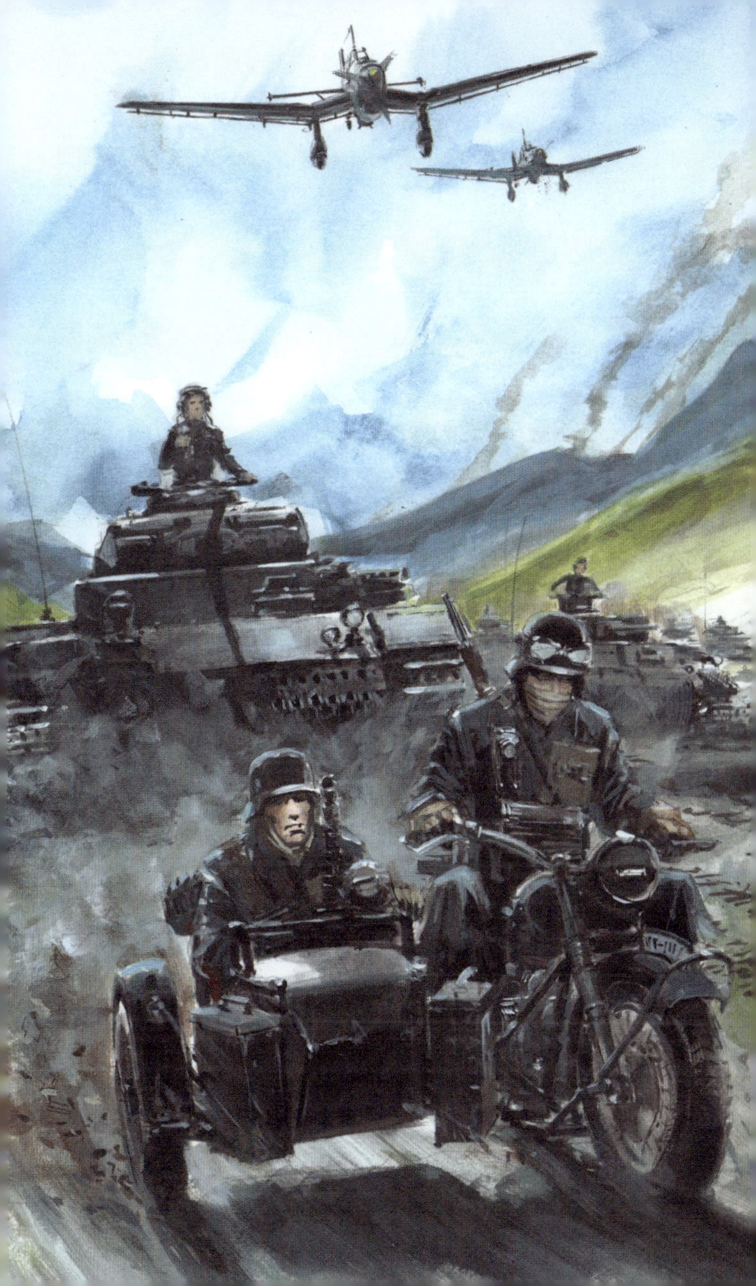

Von Manstein's plan might not have been so very original, but just how it was to be carried out most certainly was, and for that the man responsible above all others was General Guderian. Aged fifty-one, he was a deep thinker on military matters and had even published a book, *Achtung Panzer!*, about the use of tanks in modern warfare. He was breathing new life into the old principles of *Bewegungskrieg*.

It was widely accepted, though, in the German Army and in other countries too, that tanks could not be used without the support of the infantry. Britain and France had developed armoured divisions made up almost entirely of tank units, which would then operate alongside infantry divisions. Guderian, however, was creating something quite different. A panzer division included not just tanks but also motorized infantry and motorized artillery. In other words, it was a mechanized formation of all arms. Tanks, infantry and artillery could then move together and operate together, offering mutual support in one self-contained unit. What's more, they could keep in communication by radio, liberally spread throughout every part of the division. It was this ability to communicate with each component that was so crucial. Radios gave the division enormous flexibility and, with it, speed of manoeuvre.

Training together was also crucial, but it was this speed of operations that Guderian thought would give them a significant edge because he knew from intelligence that the French operated far more slowly.

General Guderian in his command vehicle standing over radio and Enigma code-machine operators.

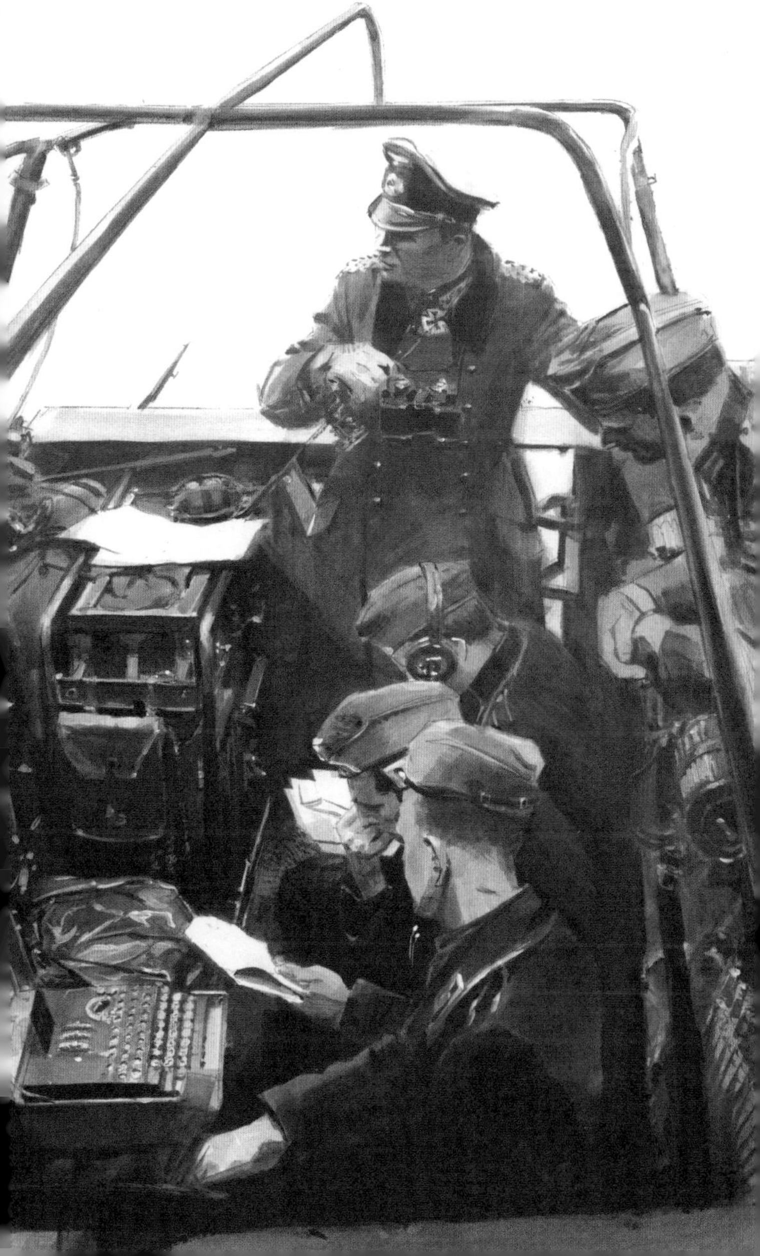

Even so, the numbers of mechanized divisions available for the spearhead was small. In fact, just sixteen of the 135 earmarked for the attack in the west were motorized, of which only ten were panzer. None the less, Guderian reckoned these sixteen elite divisions would be enough to create the vital breakthrough. The key, he believed, was for the leading divisions to get through the Ardennes and reach the River Meuse, the principal French defensive position along that part of the front, in just three days, and cross it in four.

If they could achieve that, then he knew they could break through the main French line of defence and get in behind them before the enemy could organize itself into a coordinated counter-attack. They could round up and defeat the French bit by bit and so ensure that at the point of attack they would have superior numbers. The crucial thing was to ensure the French were unable to mass their reserves together.

Senior commanders in the German Army who both understood and believed in the kind of panzer tactics Guderian was advocating were few and far between. However, as Halder now realized, this plan was the only one offering even a chance of a decisive victory, and because it was also supported by the Führer it was the one adopted. Even so, it remained a massive all-or-nothing gamble and its chances of success depended on a great deal that could very easily go wrong.

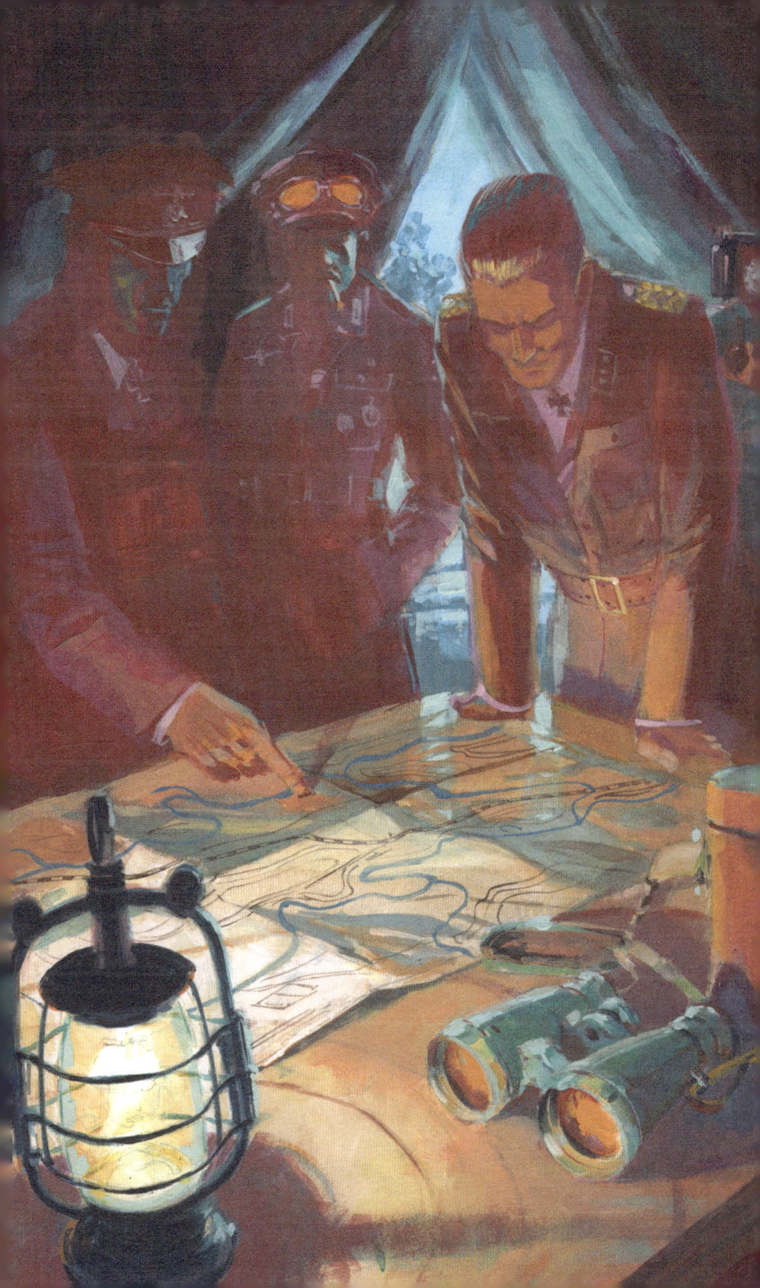

In the meantime, though, Hitler also announced plans to attack Denmark and Norway, and to do so before an attack in the west. This made little sense. Far more logical would be to attack France and the Low Countries first. If they were successful, then they would be able to walk into Norway almost unopposed: France would already have been vanquished and Britain at the very least in no position to fight. But by attacking Denmark and Norway first, Hitler risked losing precious men and materiel just before the greatest clash of arms yet faced by the Wehrmacht.

As it happened, since the previous autumn Britain and France had been debating the possibility of a pre-emptive strike on Norway and Sweden. Nearly all Germany's iron ore came from northern Sweden and was mostly shipped out through the northern Norwegian port of Narvik. However, the Allies could not agree on the right plan, nor were they willing to risk Scandinavian hostility. Not until early April did they finally decide to mine the Leads, the waters off Narvik.

By coincidence, Allied warships were sailing towards the Leads at exactly the same time as the Germans were launching their invasion of Denmark and Norway. German naval forces were spotted steaming up the Norwegian coast on 7 April, prompting frantic recalculations from the British. Next day, HMS *Glowworm*, a British destroyer, intercepted the German heavy cruiser *Admiral Hipper* and four destroyers. After being repeatedly hit, and with her decks on fire, *Glowworm* in an heroic final act rammed the *Admiral Hipper*, shearing off 40 metres of the cruiser's prow. Moments later, *Glowworm* rolled, then blew up.

Then, early on 9 April, Germany invaded both Denmark and southern Norway simultaneously, using air and naval forces, and both ground and airborne troops.

HMS *Glowworm* rams the *Admiral Hipper*.

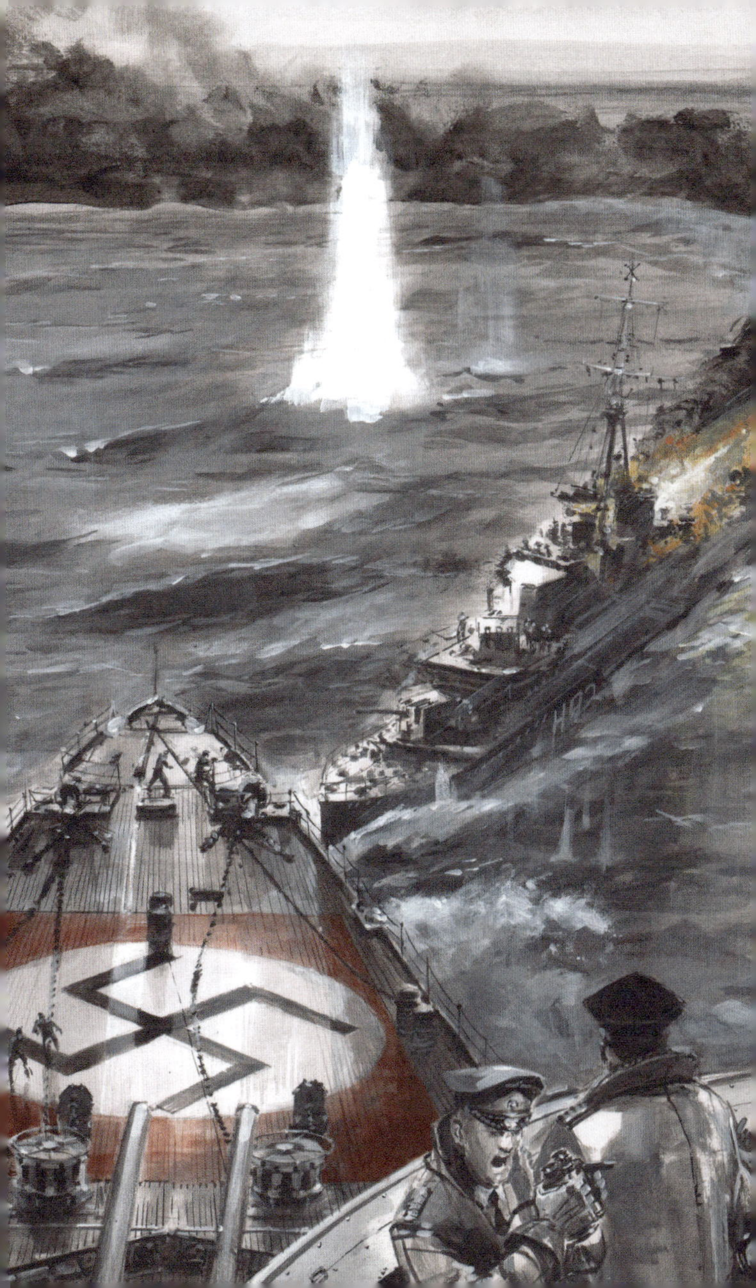

Despite the questionable strategy, the German invasion of Denmark and Norway was none the less brilliantly planned and executed. Denmark fell in a matter of hours as German *Fallschirmjäger* dropped from the sky in what was the first ever use of paratroopers in action. At the same time, ground troops stormed ashore in five simultaneous landings. In Norway, further airborne troops and landings, supported by large numbers of air forces, also quickly overwhelmed any resistance. Oslo, the capital, fell that day, 9 April.

Britain hurriedly sent reinforcements, but they lacked support from the air as well as any heavy firepower, and, despite trying to meet the German drive northwards, were soon pushed back. Only at Narvik, in the far north, was a joint British and French force successful. Eventually, however, in June, they were compelled to evacuate even this small foothold. On the ground, and with much shorter lines of supply than the Allies, the Germans swiftly swept over most of the country.

At sea, however, it was a very different story. The size and training of the Royal Navy soon inflicted a hammer-blow on the German Navy, the Kriegsmarine: half the German destroyer force was sunk, as were one of two heavy cruisers, two of six light cruisers and six U-boats. Other vessels were badly damaged, leaving Germany with a much-depleted navy capable of achieving little. On top of that, the Luftwaffe lost 242 aircraft in the campaign – machines and crew that would be needed in the summer to come.

German destroyers sinking at Narvik.

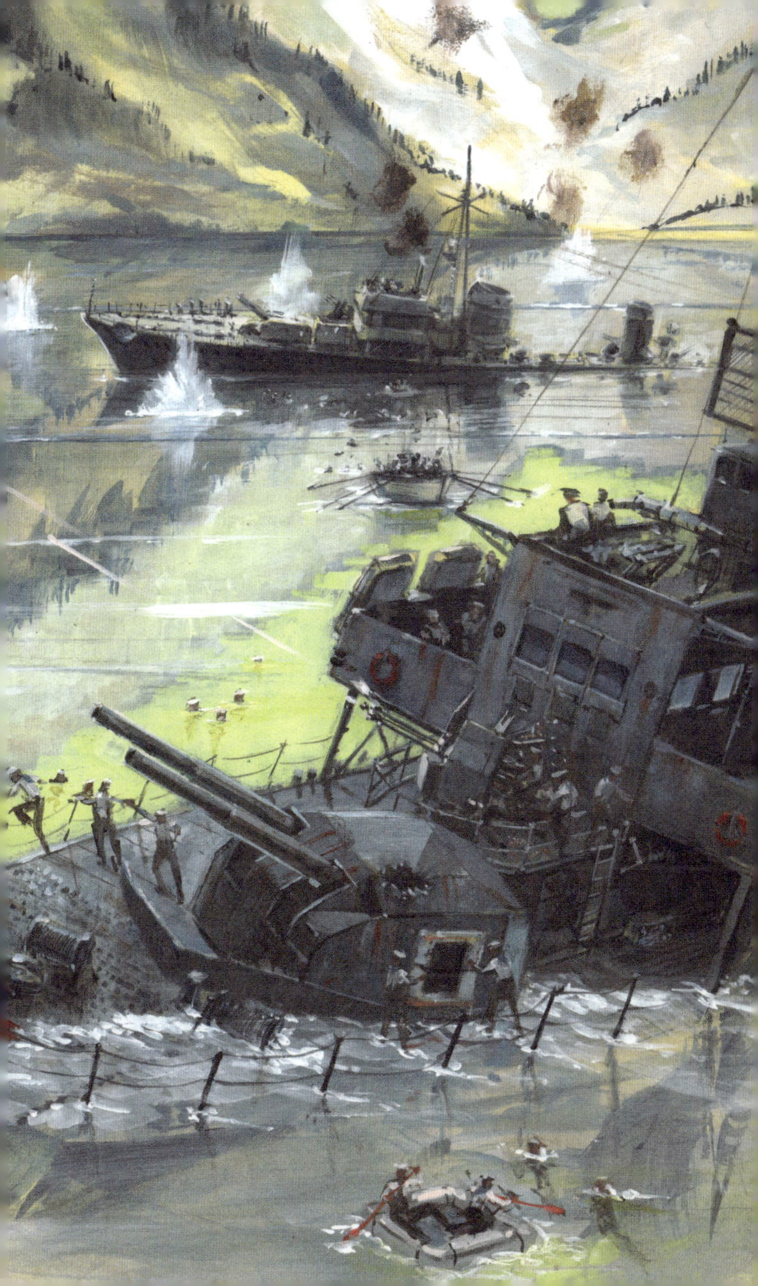

The Germans finally launched their attack on the West early on Friday 10 May 1940. The bulk of the Luftwaffe attacked targets in support of the northern thrust of Army Group B through the Netherlands and Belgium, while airborne troops parachuted down to capture key bridges and, in the first-ever glider-borne operation, the important Belgian fort of Eben-Emael was swiftly taken too.

As the Germans had hoped, the French and British immediately started moving from their positions in northern France into Belgium to meet the attack. Belgium had been neutral and had refused to allow French and British troops on to their soil before Germany made any attack. This meant these troops now had to travel up to 80 miles to the River Dyle, where they planned to link up with Dutch and Belgian forces and make their main stand. In all, twenty-five French and five British divisions began moving north, albeit slowly. The first British troops did not cross into Belgium until 10.20 a.m., nearly four hours after first being ordered to do so. Furthermore, the roads were already beginning to clog with fleeing civilians heading in the opposite direction. This was something none of the Allied war leaders had considered beforehand. It was already looking like quite a bad oversight.

Meanwhile, across the Channel in London, the British Prime Minister, Neville Chamberlain, had been forced to resign over Britain's failure in Norway. At this moment of extreme crisis, Winston Churchill, seen by many as a dangerous maverick with poor judgement, took over the reins.

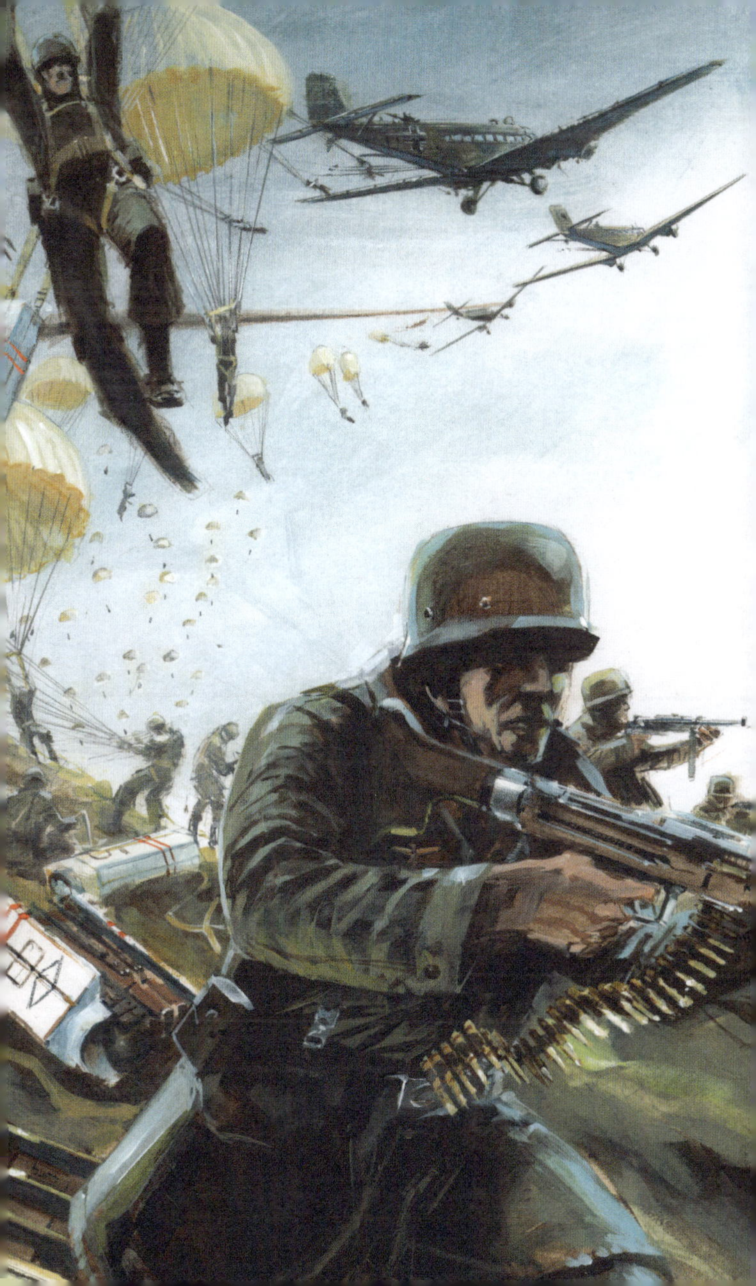

While British and French troops moved into the Low Countries, the main German thrust by Army Group A began its drive through the Ardennes. Leading the advance was Guderian's panzer corps of three divisions, heading to Sedan. To help them reach the Meuse in only three days, the troops were given an amphetamine called Pervitin to keep them awake and were told to keep going at all costs. They had 100 miles and six major obstacles to overcome: the Luxembourg border, two lines of Belgian defences, then the River Semois, the French border posts, and finally the River Meuse, the French main line of defence.

Meanwhile, following behind Guderian was a second panzer corps, under General Georg-Hans Reinhardt, which was to cross the Meuse 25 miles to the north at Monthermé, while a further 20 miles north from there, two more panzer divisions were to get across the Meuse at Dinant. Once over, these three thrusts were to advance rapidly and link up, then wait for the infantry to catch up. Then, with the bulk of the northern Allied forces facing Army Group B, the southern thrust would sweep west behind them and catch them in an enormous encirclement. There remained, however, much that could go wrong.

In fact, the plan was already beginning to unravel because behind Guderian's troops were almost 40,000 of Army Group A's vehicles, as well as infantry divisions now cutting across Panzer Corps Reinhardt's advance. The roads were narrow and few and far between. Gridlock ensued.

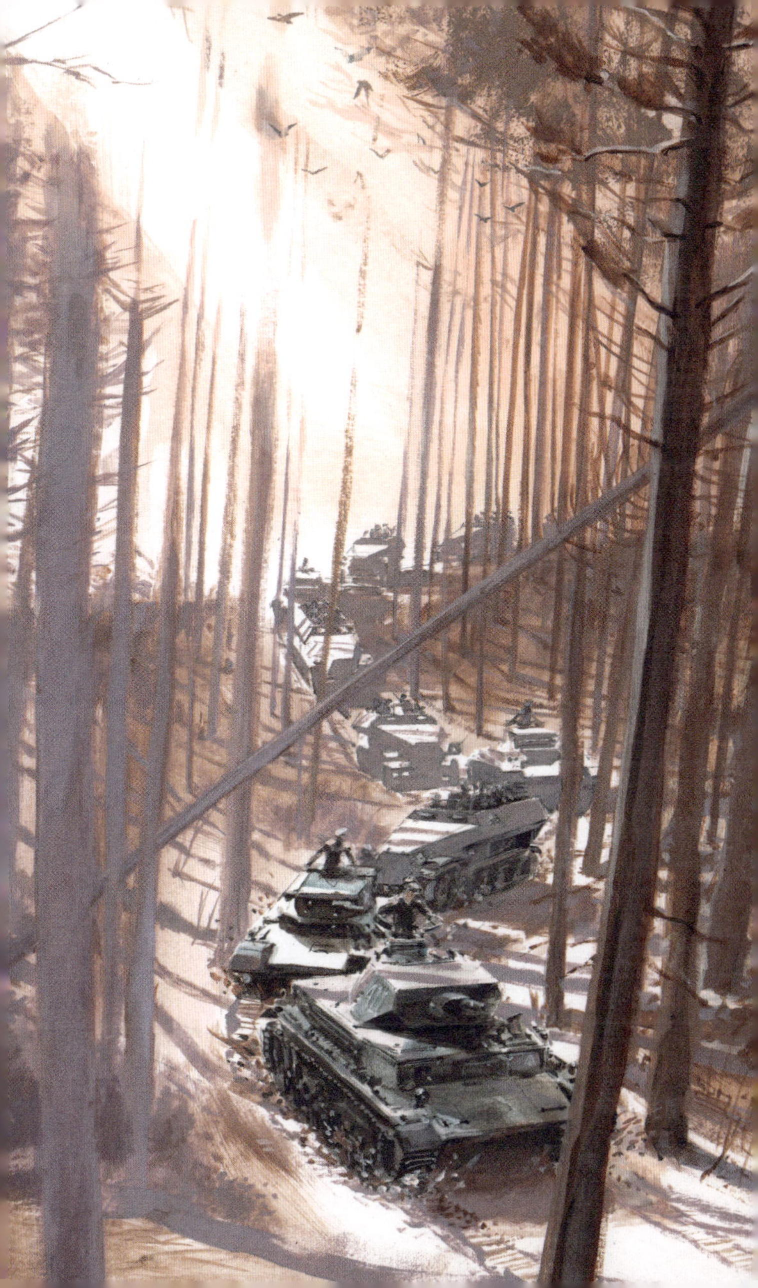

Tragically for the Allies, although aerial reconnaissance spotted this vast traffic jam, the information was dismissed by the French 9th Army intelligence section as impossible. As a result, the opportunity to mass-bomb much of Army Group A while they were sitting ducks was not taken.

Meanwhile, Guderian's lead troops reached Sedan, as planned, on the afternoon of 12 May. Sedan lay on the hinge of the French defences. To the south, along the Franco-German border, were the forts, tunnels and bunkers of the Maginot Line. To the north-west, however, was the Belgian border and from here French and British troops were swinging north towards the Dyle. Sedan had been crossed by German troops in 1870 and again in 1914, and in 1917 it had been in German hands and the site of a war school, which Guderian had attended. He knew the area well.

His troops attacked across the Meuse in three places on 13 May. French defences were weak, the Luftwaffe struck in force, and Guderian's infantry were able to storm the river and smash the French bunkers. By nightfall on the 13th, Sedan had fallen and the French were on the run. French tanks waiting in reserve were slow to move and by the following morning, with the first panzers now across the river, they were caught in a trap and destroyed.

Meanwhile, at Monthermé, just enough of Reinhardt's troops had miraculously reached the Meuse and crossed on the 13th too, while at Dinant, Major-General Erwin Rommel's 7th Panzer and the 5th Panzer Division also attacked successfully across the river.

A half-track of the 1st Panzer Division advancing through Sedan.

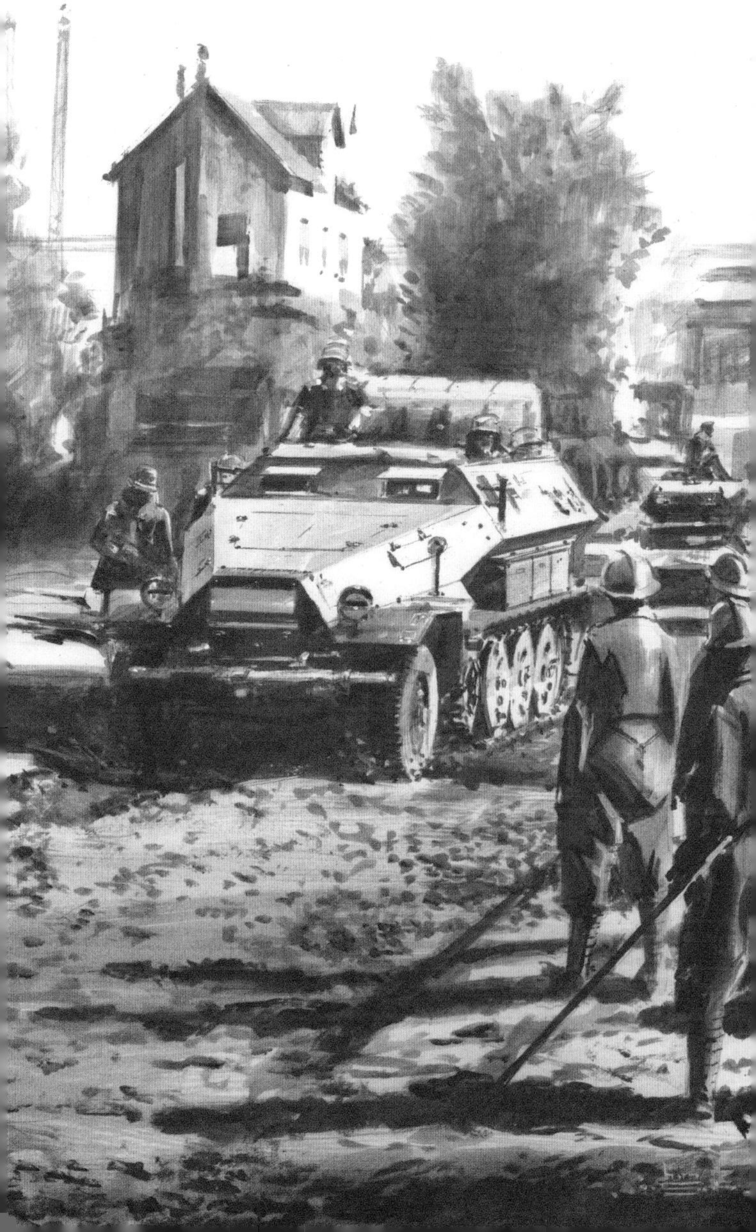

These attacking troops were the best-trained and most motivated in the German Army and, although they were by no means representative of the whole – only around 38 per cent of the army was fully trained – the achievement of this spearhead was extraordinary and a masterpiece example of *Bewegungskrieg*. None the less, the French defenders should have been able to stop them. The trouble was, many of the French senior commanders were too old and too stuck in the doctrine of the past, and so believed this new war would be much like the last, with little movement. They had believed it would take the Germans two weeks to reach their main line of defence, not three days. And although the French were bristling with double the number of guns and bigger, better tanks than the Germans, they lacked radios. Communications depended on land lines, which were all too quickly cut by bombing, and dispatch riders who got nowhere on roads now choked with refugees.

The inability of the French to move swiftly was demonstrated horribly on 15 May when the 1st Armoured Division came up against Rommel's 7th Panzer and the 5th Panzer Division. The French 1st Armoured began the day with 176 tanks, but by nightfall had just thirty-six left. By the following morning there were only sixteen. Although French tanks were superior, the Germans, using radio, were able to lure them into hidden screens of high-velocity anti-tank guns. In this way, the crème de la crème of the French Army was destroyed.

Knocked-out Char Bs of the French 1st Armoured Division.

YSEP

The entire French front along the Meuse had collapsed. French troops had been trained to hold a fixed position. They had not been encouraged to use their initiative and so now did not know what to do. Many simply put their hands in the air and surrendered.

The French leaders were caught like rabbits in headlights. Panic set in as the scale of the catastrophe swiftly sank in. General Alphonse Georges, the French commander in the north, visited British headquarters and burst into tears. It did little to help matters.

In the north, the Dutch surrendered on 15 May. That same day, the French Prime Minister, Paul Reynaud, called Churchill and said, 'We have been defeated.' Then he paused and added, 'We have been beaten; we have lost the battle.' He was quite right. Momentum was with the Germans and the French were unable to respond swiftly enough to mount the kind of rapid and concentrated counter-attack needed. How could they when orders were taking up to twelve hours to get through and sometimes even longer?

Meanwhile, the panzer divisions were ignoring the orders of their senior commanders to wait for the infantry and instead continued their drive west. 'Keep going, don't look left or right,' Rommel told his men. 'The enemy is confused. We must take advantage of it.' Guderian was urging his men to do the same: 'Hit hard, not softly!'

On 20 May, just ten days after setting out from the German border, the first of Guderian's troops reached the Atlantic coast near Abbeville.

The great gamble had paid off.

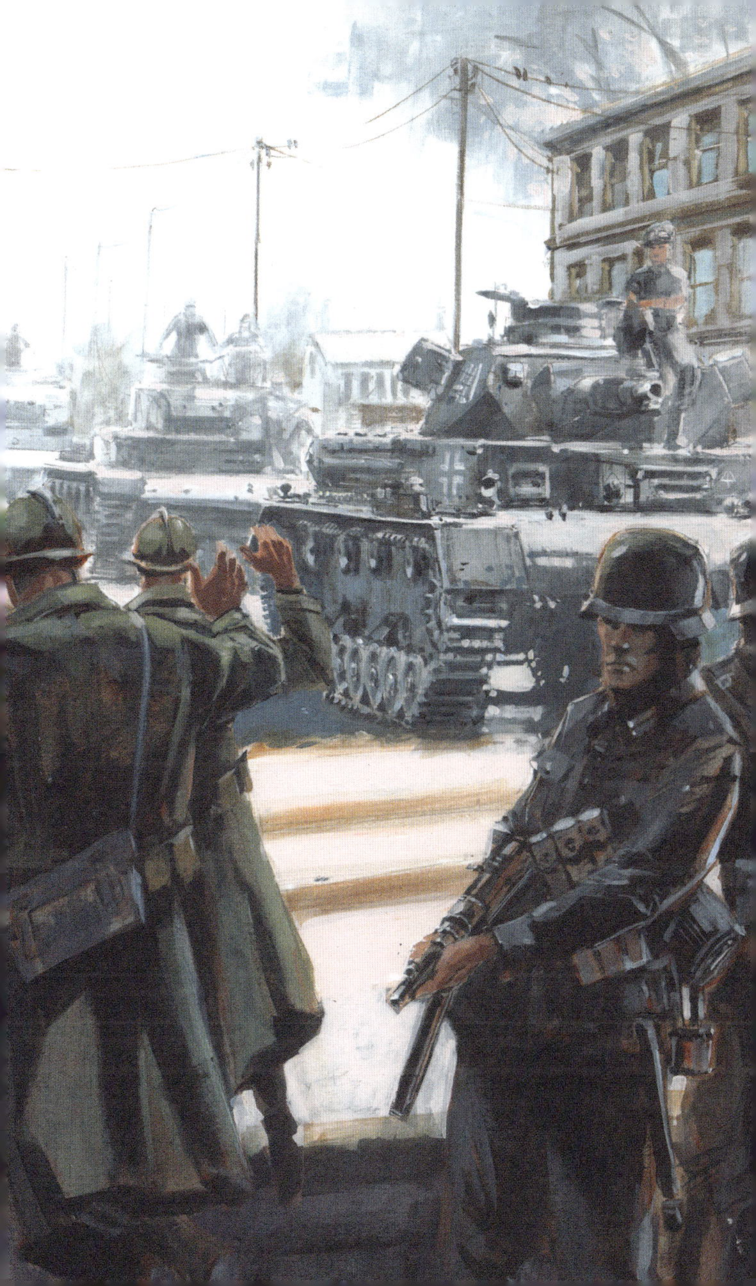

Following the Dutch surrender, Belgian, British and French troops began falling back to the next defensive line along the River Escaut, 40 miles to the west, along roads heaving with refugees. The Luftwaffe bombed and machine-gunned at will, and also hit Allied airfields, where, without radar or any early-warning system, many aircraft were destroyed on the ground.

The bulk of the Allied forces were now trapped in a large, narrow corridor and the danger was that all too soon German troops would encircle them entirely and cut them off from the Channel coast.

On 19 May, General Maurice Gamelin was sacked as commander-in-chief, but replaced with an even older man, General Maxime Weygand, aged seventy-three. Meanwhile, the British had demanded a major joint Anglo-French counter-attack with simultaneous strikes from south and north in an effort to drive a wedge through the advancing panzers. On 21 May, the British attacked Rommel's troops southwards to the west of Arras, but only a handful of French joined them and none at all attacked from the south. The Arras counter-attack proved to be little more than a demonstration in force.

Even so, Rommel himself had thought the situation so desperate that he took personal command of some anti-tank guns. It suggested a major blow might have been achieved had the French been able to organize themselves more quickly. As it was, the failure of the counter-attack signalled the last hope for the northern Allied armies.

Rommel directs the fire of a battery of 88mm guns during the British counter-attack at Arras.

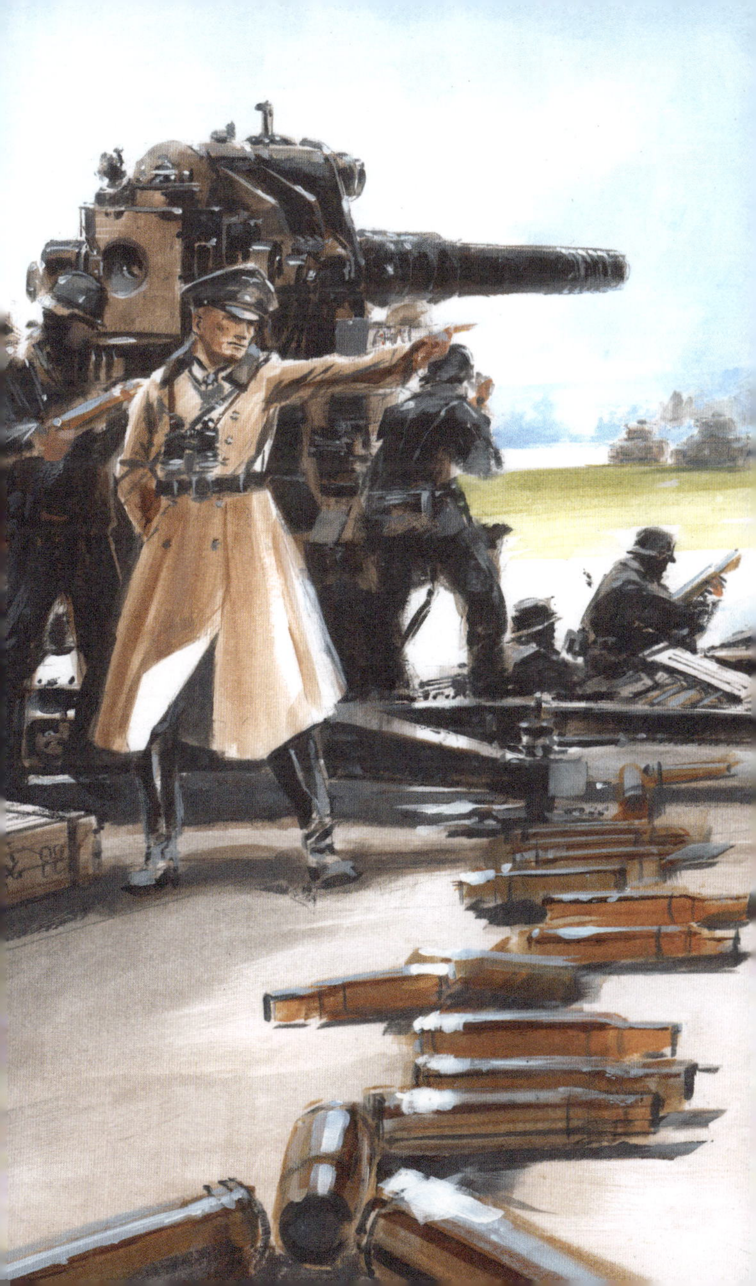

The Allied troops were still corralled in a long, narrow wedge of Flanders, which had become a corridor of military failure and civilian misery. General Weygand now ordered a second major counter-attack, but General Lord John Gort, the commander of the British Expeditionary Force, had already decided there was only one option left: to try to evacuate as many troops as possible from the Channel ports while they still had the chance.

At this point, the British were offered an unexpected lifeline. Field Marshal Gerd von Rundstedt, the commander of Army Group A, had been shocked by the Arras counter-attack and now ordered his panzer divisions to halt to allow the infantry to catch up. Halder, realizing they had a golden chance to neatly trap all the northern Allied armies, immediately countermanded this. When Hitler found out what Halder had done, however, he chose to berate the army chief of staff and sided with von Rundstedt. Thus the panzers remained halted, although by this time both Boulogne and Calais had fallen. Only Dunkirk remained in Allied hands.

When Gort learned about this order, he immediately called on the Royal Navy to put Operation DYNAMO, the naval evacuation of the BEF, into effect, although he did so with little optimism; he suspected only a fraction would be successfully brought home.

Back in Britain, on Sunday 26 May, King George VI called a National Day of Prayer. Few could believe the scale of the defeat.

The withdrawal of the BEF, 28-29 May 1940.

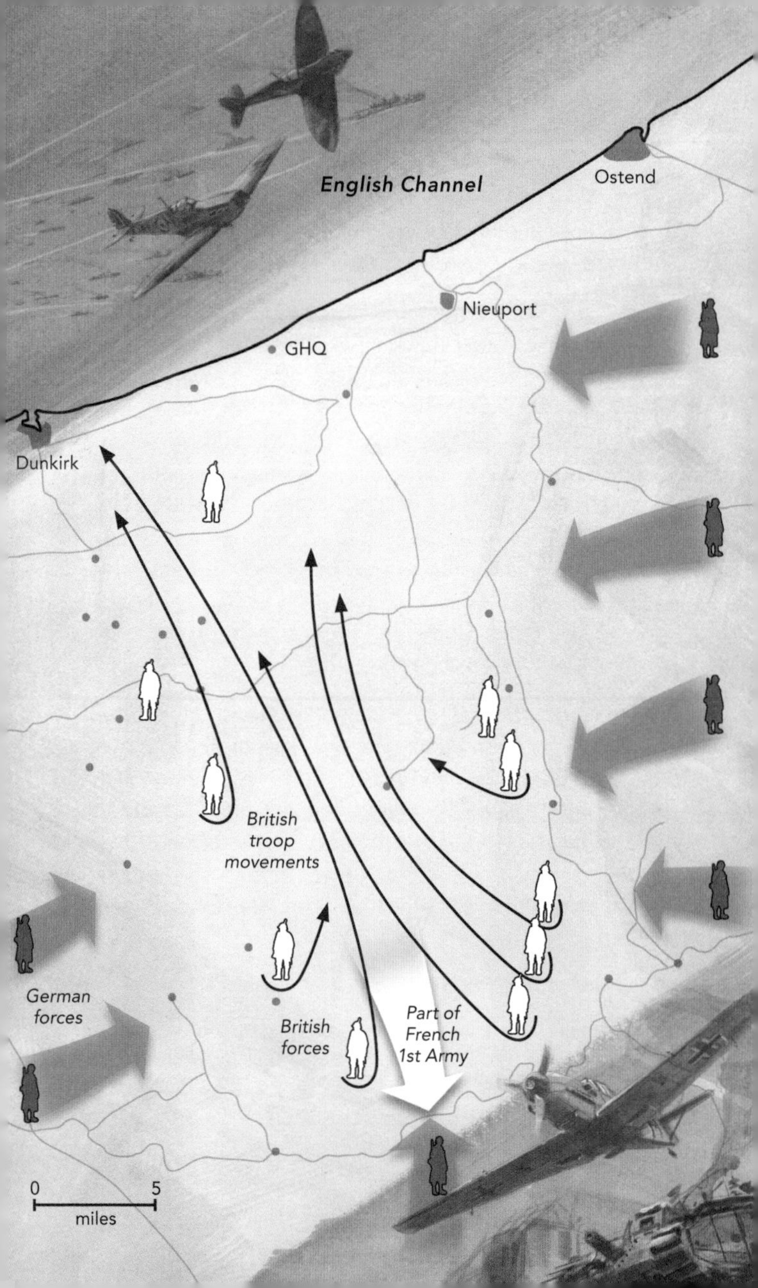

English Channel
Ostend
Nieuport
GHQ
Dunkirk
British troop movements
German forces
British forces
Part of French 1st Army
0
5
miles

Sunday 26 May was also the first day of the evacuation and a mere 7,669 men were safely lifted from the beaches. None the less, while some units were ordered to make for Dunkirk, others were fiercely defending a rapidly shrinking corridor. It was these actions that enabled the bulk of the BEF to fall behind a defensive perimeter of canals around Dunkirk.

It was Hitler's determination to show the army command who was boss, rather than any good military sense, that made him insist on the halt order. By the time it was lifted and the panzers began moving again on the morning of 27 May, the Royal Navy had discovered that a narrow wooden mole, or jetty, at the end of the wrecked Dunkirk harbour could support ships. What's more, the weather had turned and the low cloud, combined with thick plumes of smoke from burning fuel stores, made it very difficult for the Luftwaffe successfully to attack the evacuation below. Also now helping were RAF Fighter Command's Spitfires and Hurricanes, flying over from southern England.

On 28 May, Belgium surrendered, leaving a dangerous gap in the northern part of the line. In a daring and brilliantly executed night march, however, General Bernard Montgomery's 4th Division moved overnight to plug the hole and a crisis was prevented. At the same time, Churchill managed to avert a major argument in his War Cabinet. There would be no suing for peace, as Lord Halifax had suggested. Britain would fight on.

British troops trying to escape to HMS *Icarus* from the beaches of Dunkirk.

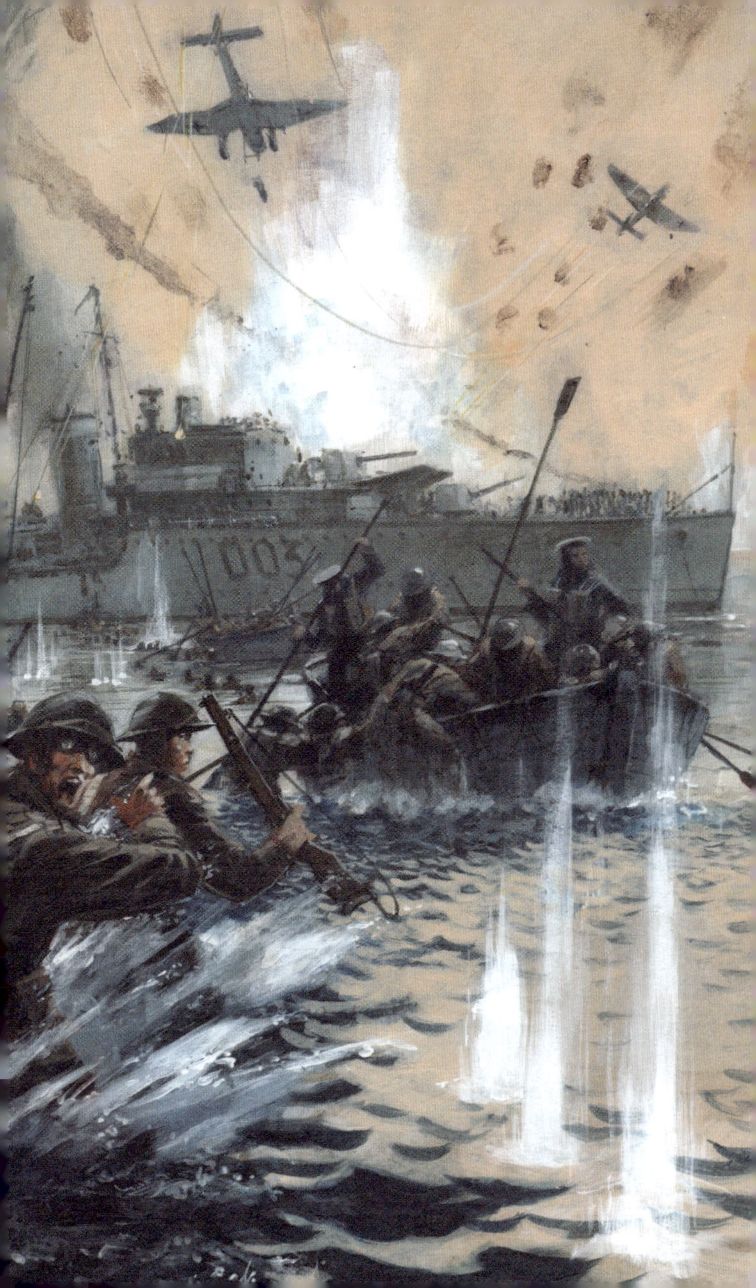

With dykes broken, fields waterlogged and determined resistance from British and French troops around the Dunkirk perimeter, the Germans found progress much harder. All the while, more and more men were being evacuated: by naval vessels, civilian cross-Channel steamers and even a mass of 'little boats' that answered the call and hurried across the Channel to help.

On 29 May, 53,823 men were lifted; the next day, 68,014 made it home. By 2 June, all British troops had been successfully picked up and then French troops were taken to England too. By 4 June, when Dunkirk finally fell, an incredible 338,226 men had been evacuated. Most of the equipment was left behind, along with some 70,000 casualties, but the bulk of the BEF's troops had been saved.

The same could not be said for the French, who were now resigned to their fate. The Germans swept southwards. Paris, the capital, fell on 14 June, by which time Paul Reynaud had lost the support of his government and his senior commanders. Both Weygand and Marshal Philippe Pétain, the hero of the great French defensive victory at Verdun back in 1916, had given up and were demanding an armistice. Churchill and his senior advisors urged the French to fight on, but Reynaud had been right: the battle had been all but lost the moment the Meuse front had collapsed.

The French, who had shed so much blood and fought with such iron determination a generation earlier, no longer had the heart to do so again.

While British troops were evacuated from Dunkirk, nearly all their heavy equipment was abandoned.

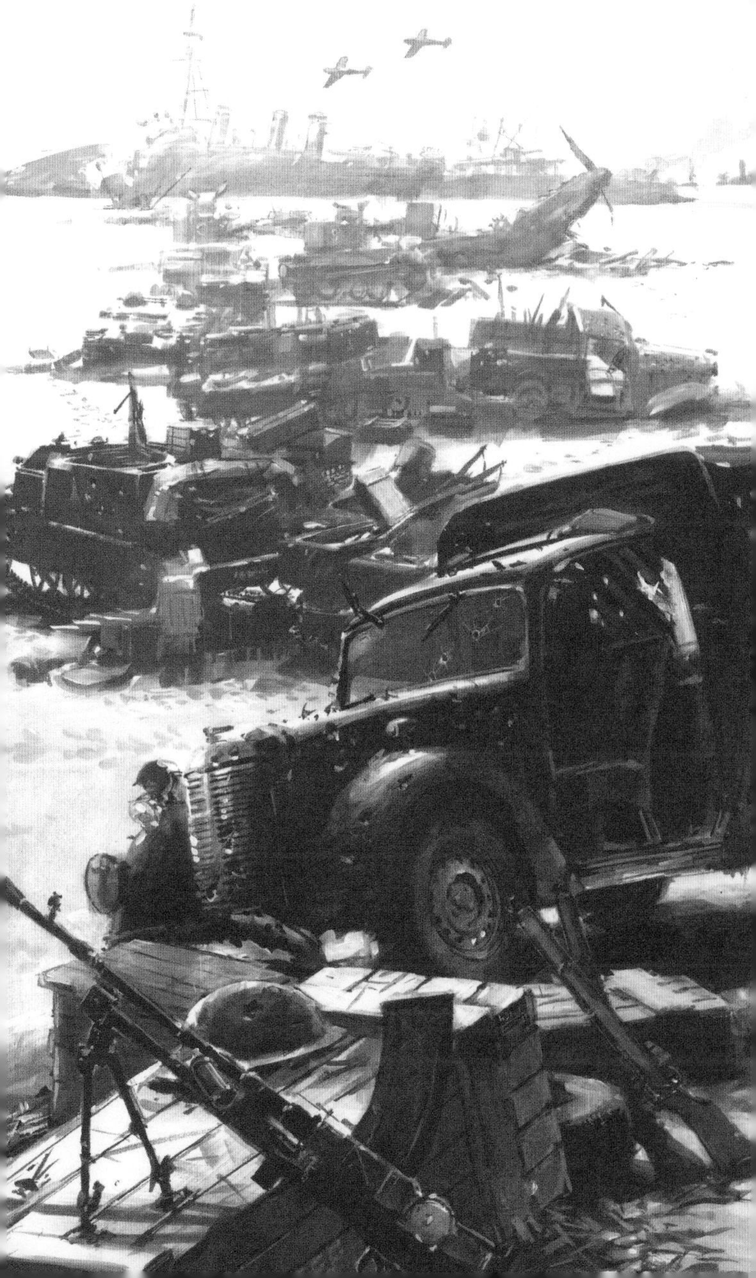

The French armistice was signed on 22 June in the same railway carriage in Compiègne in which the Germans had surrendered in 1918. For Hitler, who was there to witness France's humiliation, there could be no sweeter moment of victory.

Their success, however, was as much about French failures as it was about German brilliance, and the facts remained that German losses in the air had been high and the bulk of the damage had been accomplished by a very small proportion of the army. If Germany could continue to defeat her enemies in campaigns of only a few weeks, then their lack of resources would not matter very much.

On the other hand, Britain was still in the war and had been given a lifeline by Hitler's own ego and incompetence. Without the halt order, it is hard to see how so many could possibly have escaped. What's more, Britain lay across the sea, with her mighty navy and merchant fleet and with a growing air force protected by the world's only fully coordinated air defence system. *Bewegungskrieg* – which was now becoming known as 'Blitzkrieg' – would not work on water or in the air alone. Thus, for all the brilliance of the German victory in the west, the war was not over yet, not while Britain fought on. Despite its successes, in its failure to defeat Britain the Blitzkrieg had fallen short.

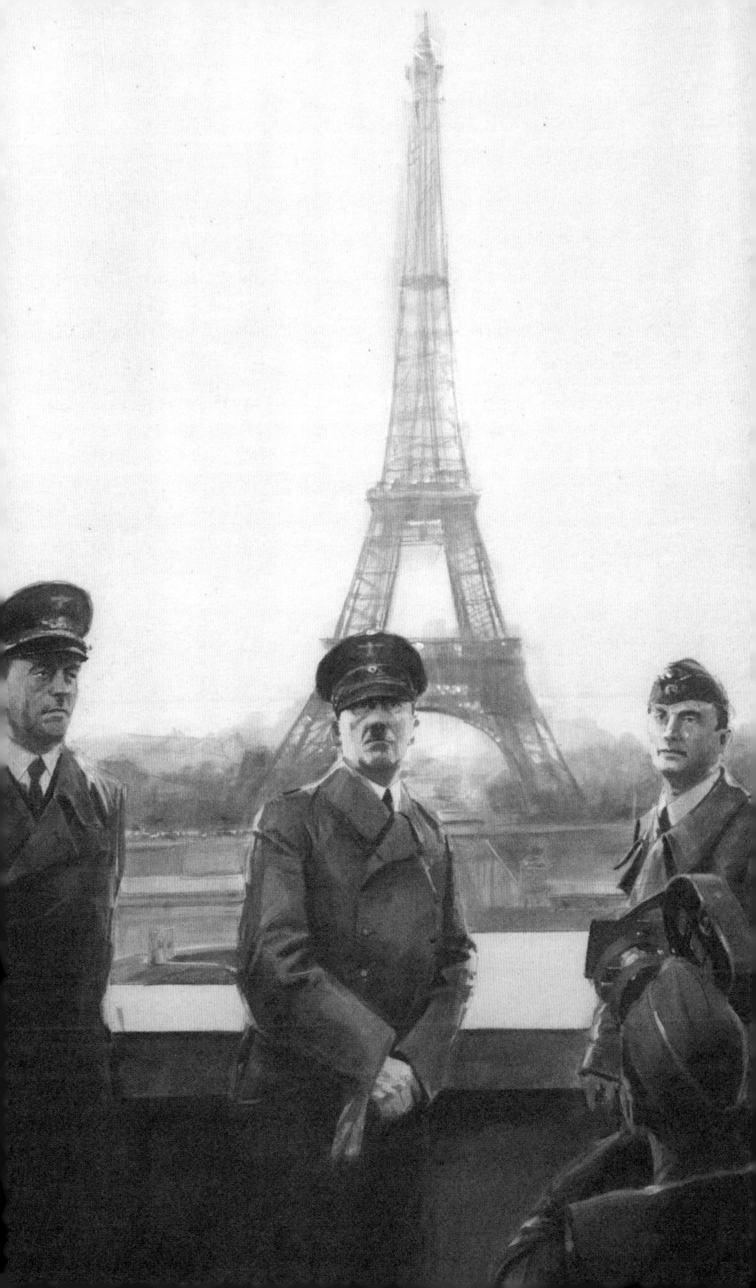

Further Reading

GENERAL HISTORIES

Robert M. Citino *The German Way of War* (University Press of Kansas, 2005)

Phil Craig and Tim Clayton *Finest Hour* (Coronet, 2001)

Karl-Heinz Frieser *The Blitzkrieg Legend* (Naval Institute Press, 2013)

James Holland *The War in the West: The Rise of Germany, 1939–1941* (Corgi, 2016)

James Holland *Battle of Britain* (Corgi, 2011)

Alistair Horne *To Lose a Battle* (Penguin Books, 1990)

MEMOIRS

Heinz Guderian *Panzer Leader* (Penguin Books, 2000)

Hans von Luck *Panzer Commander* (Cassell, 2002)

NOVELS

James Holland *Darkest Hour* (Corgi, 2010)

James Holland *Duty Calls: Dunkirk* (Puffin, 2011)